THE LITTLE
BLACK BOOK

DIRTY
JOKE

A Collection of
Common Indecencies

COMPILED BY EVELYN BEILENSON

ILLUSTRATED BY RICHARD A. GOLDBERG

PETER PAUPER PRESS, INC.
WHITE PLAINS, NEW YORK

Most of these jokes are from the book:
The Mammoth Book of Dirty, Sick, X-Rated &
Politically Incorrect Jokes by Geoff Tibballs
Copyright © 2005 by Geoff Tibballs
Appears by permission of the publisher, Carroll & Graf,
A Division of Avalon Publishing Group, Inc.

Designed by Heather Zschock

Illustrations copyright © 2007
Richard A. Goldberg

Copyright © 2007
Peter Pauper Press, Inc.
202 Mamaroneck Avenue
White Plains, NY 10601
All rights reserved
ISBN 978-1-59359-860-0
Printed in Hong Kong
7 6 5 4 3 2 1

Visit us at www.peterpauper.com

THE LITTLE
BLACK BOOK OF
DIRTY
JOKES

CONTENTS

introduction

This *Little Black Book of Dirty Jokes* is just the key to release your inner animal . . . you know, the one that wants to guffaw in polite company, the one that refuses to sit with legs crossed, the one that laughs at common decency! We all know you didn't leave sophomoric humor behind when you left school. So here is a collection worthy of any tasteless house party, golf outing, or girls' night on the town. We're talking lusty humor here; we're talking unadulterated lewdness.

No one escapes the gritty pages of this hilarious and raunchy collection—from doctors and ministers to donkeys and octogenarians. Divided for convenience into chapters featuring Gross Anatomy, Oral Agreements, and the like, this smutty little book serves up obscene amounts of fodder. Large enough to contain hundreds of jokes, but small enough to easily be hidden from the kids, here's your ticket to titillation!

jokes

MARRIAGE

A married couple was lying in bed at night. The wife had settled down ready to go to sleep, but the husband was reading a book by the light of his bedside lamp. As he was reading, he paused momentarily, reached over to his wife and started fondling her pussy before resuming reading his book.

Aroused by his touch, she got out of bed and slipped off her nightdress.

The husband was mystified. "What are you doing?" he asked.

"You were playing with my pussy," replied the wife. "I thought it was foreplay for something heavier."

The husband exclaimed: "Hell no! I was just wetting my fingers so I could turn the pages."

A biker and his wife were celebrating their fiftieth wedding anniversary. That night, she entered the bedroom wearing the same sexy little negligee that she had worn on their wedding night. She said, "Honey, do you remember this?"

"Yeah," he said. "You were wearing that on the night we married."

"That's right," she smiled. "And do you remember what you said to me that night?"

"Yeah, I said: 'Baby, I'm going to suck the life out of those big tits and screw your brains out.'"

She giggled and said: "That's exactly what you said. So now it's fifty years later, and I'm in the same negligee I wore that night. What do you have to say tonight?"

He looked her up and down and said: "Mission accomplished."

A man bought a new range of Olympic condoms. "There are three colors," he told his wife. "Gold, silver, and bronze."

"What color are you going to wear tonight?" she asked.

"Gold, of course," he replied proudly.

"Why don't you wear silver?" she asked. "It would be nice if you came second for a change."

A husband came home with half a gallon of ice cream and asked his wife if she wanted some.

"How hard is it?" she asked.

"About as hard as my dick," he replied.

"Pour me some."

Hung Chow calls into work and says, "Hey, boss, I no come work today, I really sick. I got headache, stomachache, and my legs hurt. I no come work."

The boss says, "You know, Hung Chow, I really need you today. When I feel like this I go to my wife and tell her give me sex. That makes everything better and I go work. You try that."

Two hours later Hung Chow calls again. "Boss, I do what you say and I feel great. I be at work soon. You got nice house."

A man and his wife had an argument in bed, after which he slept downstairs. The next day she felt guilty and decided to buy him a present. As he was a keen golfer, she went to the pro shop. The pro suggested a putter and showed her one of the best in stock.

"One hundred and fifty dollars," said the pro.

"That's a bit expensive."

"But it comes with an inscription."

"What kind of inscription?"

"Whatever you like, but one of the old golfers' favorites is NEVER UP, NEVER IN."

"Oh, that will do," said the wife. "After all, that's what started the argument in the first place."

Two married men were discussing their sex lives. One asked, "Does your wife ever let you do it doggie fashion?"

"Not exactly," replied the second. "She's more into doing doggy tricks."

"Wow!" said the first. "What does that entail? Sounds pretty kinky."

"Sadly, it's not," said the second. "Whenever I make a move, she rolls over and plays dead."

Three women were sitting around drinking and talking about their love lives.

Carly said: "I call my husband the dentist. Nobody can drill like he does."

Lauren giggled and confessed: "I call my husband the miner because of his incredible shaft."

All the while Maxine kept quiet until Carly asked: "What do you call your husband?"

Maxine frowned and said: "The postman—because he always delivers late, and half the time it's in the wrong box."

Two married buddies were out drinking one night. One turned to the other and said: "It's a real problem. Whenever I go home after we've been out drinking, I turn the headlights off before I get to the driveway, I shut off the engine and coast into the garage, I take my shoes off before I go into the house, I creep up the stairs, I get undressed in the bathroom, I ease gently into bed without disturbing the duvet and STILL my wife wakes up and yells at me for staying out so late!"

His buddy took a swig of beer and said: "You're doing it all wrong! I screech into the driveway, slam the door, storm up the stairs, throw my shoes into the closet, jump into bed, rub my hands on my wife's ass and say, 'How about a blow job?' . . . and she's always sound asleep."

When each of her three daughters got married, their mother asked them to write to her with the truth about their new married lives. To avoid embarrassing their respective husbands with intimate details of their sex lives, mother and daughters agreed to use newspaper advertisements as a secret code.

The first wrote back after a week of marriage with the simple message: "Maxwell House Coffee."

The mother checked the newspaper, found the Maxwell House advertisement, and was pleased to read that it said: "Good to the last drop."

The second daughter sent a message after two weeks of marriage. It read: "Rothman's Mattresses."

So the mother looked at the Rothman's Mattresses ad, and it said, "Full size, king size." Mother was happy.

Then the third daughter sent her letter after a month of marriage. It read simply: "British Airways."

Mother looked for the British Airways ad, but this time she fainted. For the ad read: "Three times a day, seven days a week, both ways."

A researcher carrying out a survey on marital sex phoned one of the participants to check on a discrepancy. He asked the husband: "In response to the question on frequency of intercourse, you answered 'once a week,' but your wife has answered 'several times a night.'"

"That's correct," said the husband. "And that's the way it's going to be until the mortgage is paid off."

A doctor was having an affair with his nurse and soon she told him she was pregnant. Not wanting his wife to know, he gave the nurse a sum of money and told her to go to Italy and have the baby there.

"But how will I let you know the baby is born?" asked the nurse.

"Just send me a postcard and write 'spaghetti' on the back."

Six months later the doctor's wife called him at the office and said that he had received a strange postcard from Europe. When the doctor arrived home that evening, he read the card and immediately collapsed onto the floor with a heart attack. While the paramedics were preparing to rush him to the hospital, one asked the wife what had precipitated the cardiac arrest. Still mystified, she picked up the card and read; "Spaghetti, Spaghetti, Spaghetti, Spaghetti—two with sausage and meatballs, two without."

An eighty-year-old rancher was about to marry a young girl of twenty-one. His trusted friend and adviser, the local banker, had serious doubts as to how long an old man would be able to satisfy such a young bride and feared for his friend's happiness. So, for the sake of matrimonial harmony, he advised the old man to bring in a hired hand to help around the ranch, knowing full well that the hired hand would probably help out in the bedroom, too, behind the old man's back. The rancher thought it was a great idea.

Four months later, the banker called on his friend. "How's your new wife?" he asked.

"She's pregnant," replied the old man.

The banker smiled knowingly. "And how's the hired hand?"

"Oh, she's pregnant, too!"

An old man was proudly displaying his physique to his wife. "What do you think of my balls?" he asked. "Still pretty big, huh? I think of them as my Crown Jewels."

"Yes," said the wife. "They're for display purposes only."

When a sixty-eight-year-old millionaire married a twenty-year-old model, his friend was understandably envious. "You lucky devil," he said. "How did you manage to get such a beautiful young wife?"

"Easy," replied the millionaire. "I simply told her I was ninety-six."

A guy was asked why he married a sadist. He said: "Beats me!"

A man and his wife were having sex. Fifteen minutes passed, then thirty, then forty-five. The sweat was pouring off them and it was becoming increasingly apparent that neither was going to reach orgasm.

Finally the wife said: "What's the matter, darling, can't you think of anyone else either?"

Leaving their wedding reception, a young honeymoon couple hailed a cab to take them to their country hotel. The driver wasn't sure how to get there and said he'd ask for directions when they got nearer to their destination. Meanwhile the lovers started getting really passionate in the back seat.

Seeing a fork in the road, the driver said: "I take the next turn, right?"

"No way," panted the groom. "Get your own. This one's all mine."

A guy on a business trip bought a cool pair of snakeskin boots. When he got home, he went upstairs, stripped naked except for his boots, and called his wife. She entered the bedroom to find him standing there.

"Do you notice anything special?" he asked.

"Yeah," she said, bored. "It's limp."

"It's not limp," he protested. "It's admiring my new boots."

"Well," she said, "next time buy a hat."

The wife asked her husband to go to the video store and pick up "Scent of a Woman." He came home with "A Fish Called Wanda."

HANKY PANKY

Arriving home from a shopping trip, a wife was horrified to find her husband in bed with a pretty girl. Just as the wife was about to storm out of the house, her husband called out: "Before you go, I want you to hear how all this came about. Driving home, I saw this young girl, looking poor and tired. I offered her a ride. She was hungry, so I brought her home and fed her some of the roast you had forgotten about in the refrigerator. Her shoes were worn out, so I gave her a pair of your shoes that you don't wear because they are out of fashion. She was cold, so I gave her the new birthday sweater you never wear because the color doesn't suit you. Her trousers had holes in them, so I gave her a pair of yours that don't fit you anymore. Then, as this poor girl was about to leave the house, she paused and asked, 'Is there anything else that your wife doesn't use anymore?' . . . So here we are!"

A guy arrived home from work to find a stranger screwing his wife.

"What the hell are you two doing?" demanded the husband.

His wife turned to the stranger and said, "See, I told you he was stupid."

A guy walked into a bar, ordered a double scotch and moaned to the bartender: "An irate husband has written to me, threatening to have me killed unless I stop screwing his wife."

"So why don't you just stop?"

"It's not as easy as that," replied the guy. "He didn't sign his name."

A wife arrived home flashing a new diamond ring. "Where did you get that?" asked her husband suspiciously.

She said: "My boss and I played the lotto and we won, so I bought the ring with my share of the winnings."

A week later, she arrived home wearing a new Italian leather coat. "Where did you get that?" asked the husband.

"My boss and I played the lotto, and guess what, we won again. So I bought the coat with my share of the winnings."

Three weeks later, she arrived home driving a new Ferrari. "Where did you get that?" asked the husband.

"My boss and I played the lotto, and you'll never believe it, but we won again. So I bought the car with my share of the winnings."

That night she asked her husband to run her

a nice warm bath, but when she went into the bathroom she found that the bath water was only a couple of inches deep.

"Why did you only run a little amount of water?" she asked.

"Well," he mumbled sourly, "we don't want you to get your lotto ticket too wet, do we?"

Exhausted from a long day at work, a business executive arrived home to find his wife in bed with a neighbor.

"That's it!" stormed the husband. "If you're in bed screwing my wife, I'm going next door to sleep with yours!"

"Go ahead," replied the neighbor. "The rest will do you good."

A couple had been married for over forty years, but with the husband in serious financial trouble, he told his wife that he was thinking of committing suicide.

"Don't worry, honey," she said reassuringly. "We're not as hard up as you think because right from the start of our marriage I've been putting aside two dollars every time we had sex. Our savings have now grown to over $100,000!"

"Oh, that's wonderful!" he exclaimed. "What an amazing woman you are! What an ingenious idea! I'm only sorry now that I didn't give you all my business!"

A salesman was on business in Las Vegas. One evening he got chatting to a woman in a bar and eventually realized that she was a hooker.

He said: "I'll give you $200 for a mediocre blow job."

"Honey," she answered, "for $200, I'll give you the blow job of a lifetime!"

"You don't understand," he said. "I'm not horny, just homesick."

Q: What are the three words you never want to hear when making love?

A: "Honey, I'm home!"

A husband arrived home early from work to find his wife in the arms of another man. He yelled at the interloper: "What right do you have to be making love to my wife?"

The lover replied: "You may as well know that I am in love with Ethel and I would like to marry her. I understand you're a gambler? Why don't you be a sport and sit down and play a game of gin rummy with me? If I lose, I'll never see her again; if you lose, you must agree to divorce her. OK?"

"All right," said the husband. "But just to make it a little more interesting, why don't we play for a dollar a point?"

When his wife went missing, her husband searched everywhere for her. As well as reporting her disappearance to the police, he contacted all her friends and family in a bid to trace her. Then two days after she had vanished, he returned home to find her standing in the bathroom.

He threw his arms around her and cried: "Where have you been? I've been worried sick."

"These four masked men kidnapped me," she said, "tied me up, and had wild sex with me for a week."

"But it's only been two days," said the husband. "What do you mean, a week?"

She answered: "I'm only here to collect my toothbrush."

A man had six children and was so proud of his achievement that, despite his wife's objections, he started calling her "mother of six," both in private and in public.

One night the couple went to a party. When the husband was ready to go home, he called out loudly: "Shall we leave now, Mother of Six?"

Irritated by his lack of discretion, his wife shouted back: "Ready when you are, Father of Four."

A man came home from work one day and his wife asked him to fix the toilet. The man said, "Who do I look like— the plumber?" and never fixed it.

The man came home the next day and his wife asked him to fix the garbage disposal. The man said, "Who do I look like—a sink specialist?" and never fixed it.

The man came home the next day and his wife asked him to fix the refrigerator. The man said, "Who do I look like—the Maytag repairman?" and never fixed it.

The man came home the next day and his wife told him she hired someone to fix the fridge, someone to fix the garbage disposal, and someone to fix the toilet. The man asked his wife how much it cost. His wife said, "I had to either bake them a cake or have sex with them." The man asked his wife, "What kind of cake did you bake them?" The wife said, "Who do I look like—Betty Crocker?"

A woman walked into a pharmacy and told the pharmacist that she needed some cyanide. The pharmacist said, "Why in the world do you need cyanide?" The woman said she needed it to poison her husband. The pharmacist's eyes got big and he said, "Lord, have mercy—I can't give you cyanide to kill your husband! That's against the law! I'll lose my license and they'll throw you and me in jail. Just leave and forget you ever came in here before I call the police."

The woman reached into her purse and pulled out a picture of her husband in bed with the pharmacist's wife. The pharmacist looked at the picture and said, "Well, now. You didn't tell me you had a prescription."

To give his wife a break during the long school holidays, a man agreed to take his young daughter in to work for the day. When they got home in the evening the little girl said: "I saw you in your office with your secretary. Why do you call her a doll?"

Aware that his wife was listening, the husband said, "Well, it's because my secretary works really hard. I'd be lost without her. I guess that's why I call her a doll."

"Oh," said the little girl. "I thought it was because she closed her eyes when you laid her on the couch."

A woman was having an affair while her husband was out at work. One day she was in bed with her boyfriend when she heard her husband's car pull into the driveway.

"Quick!" she shouted to her boyfriend. "Grab your clothes and jump out the window. My husband is home early!"

The boyfriend looked out the window and said: "I can't jump! It's raining like crazy out there and I'm naked!"

"I don't care," she insisted. "If my husband catches us, he'll kill the pair of us."

So the boyfriend grabbed his clothes and jumped from the bedroom window. When he landed, he found himself in the middle of a group of marathon runners. Hoping to blend in even though he was naked, he started running alongside them, carrying his clothes over his arm.

One of the runners asked: "Do you always run in the nude?"

Thinking on his feet, the boyfriend replied breathlessly: "Yes, always. It feels so free having the air blow over my skin while I'm running."

"Do you always run carrying your clothes on your arm?" queried the athlete.

"Oh, yes," panted the boyfriend. "That way I can get dressed at the end of the run, get in my car, and just go straight home without a shower."

"And," persisted the athlete, "do you always wear a condom when you run?"

"Only if it's raining."

SEMANTICS

Olaf and Sven were fishing one day when Sven pulled out a cigar. Finding he had no matches, he asked Olaf for a light.

"Ya, shure, I tink I haff a lighter," he replied. Then reaching into his tackle box, he pulled out a Bic lighter 10 inches long.

"Yiminy Cricket!" exclaimed Sven, taking the huge Bic lighter in his hands. "Vhere did yew git dat monster?"

"Vell," replied Olaf, "I got it from my genie."

"You haff a genie in yor tackle box?" Sven asked.

"Ya, shure. It's right here in my tackle box," says Olaf.

"Could I see him?"

So Olaf opens his tackle box and sure enough, out pops the genie. Addressing the genie, Sven says, "Hey dere! I'm a good friend of your master. Vill you grant me vun vish?"

"Yes, I will," says the genie. So Sven asks the genie for a million bucks. The genie disappears back into the tackle box leaving Sven sitting there, waiting for his million bucks.

Suddenly, the sky darkens and is filled with the sound of a million ducks flying overhead. Over the roar of the million ducks Sven yells at Olaf, "Yumpin' Yimmny. I asked for a million bucks, not a million ducks!" Olaf answers, "Ya, I forgot to tell yew da genie is hard of hearing. Do yew really tink I asked for a 10 inch Bic?"

A young businessman picked up a blonde in a bar and took her back to his place. When she saw the bedroom, she exclaimed: "Wow! A water bed! I've never had sex on a water bed before!"

As they lay down on the bed, things soon got hot. She said: "Before we go any further, don't you think we should put on some protection?"

"Good idea," he said.

So the blonde jumped up from the water bed and went into the next room. When she returned she was wearing a life jacket.

An American businessman was in Japan. He hired a local hooker and was going at it all night with her. She kept screaming "Fujifoo! Fujifoo!" which the guy took to be pleasurable.

The next day he was playing golf with his Japanese counterparts and one of them got a hole-in-one. Wanting to impress the lucky golfer, he yelled: "fujifoo!"

Confused, the Japanese golfer looked at him and asked: "What do you mean, 'wrong hole'?"

▪

Sex is the only activity where you start at the top and work your way to the bottom, while getting a raise.

CREATURE COMFORTS

A gorilla and a rhino were best friends until one day, as the rhino bent over to drink from a watering hole, the gorilla took advantage of the situation and buggered him. The rhino reacted angrily and chased the gorilla all over the game reserve. Spotting an explorer sitting in a chair and reading a newspaper, the gorilla killed him, grabbed his clothes and paper, threw the body behind a bush, and sat down in the chair to read.

Moments later, the rhino came charging onto the scene. "Excuse me," he said. "Have you seen a gorilla around here?"

Holding up the newspaper to hide his face, the gorilla replied, "What, the one that buggered a rhino by the watering hole?"

"Oh, God!" said the rhino. "Don't tell me it's in the papers already!"

When the Ark's door was closed, Noah called a meeting with all the animals. "Listen up," he said. "There will be no sex on this trip. All of you males take off your penis and hand it to my sons. I will sit at that table over there and write you a receipt. After we see land, you can get your penis back."

A week into the journey, Mr. Rabbit hopped excitedly into his wife's cage and said, "Quick! Get on my shoulders and look out the window to see if you can see land."

She got onto his shoulders but said: "Sorry, no sign of land yet."

"Damn!" he said.

This went on every day for the next week. Each day Mr. Rabbit would rush in excitedly and ask Mrs. Rabbit if she could see land yet. Each time the answer was the same. Eventually she got fed up with him. "What's wrong with you?" she asked. "You know it will rain for forty days and forty nights. Only after the water has drained will we be able to see land. Why are you acting so excited?"

"Look," said Mr. Rabbit slyly, producing a slip of paper from his pocket. "I've got the horse's receipt!"

■

Q: What did the worm say to the caterpillar?

A: "Who did you screw to get that fur coat?"

■

Q: How many animals fit into a pair of panty hose?

A: Ten piggies, two calves, one ass, hundreds of hares, and one pussy.

A Mississippi woodpecker and a Texas woodpecker were in Mississippi arguing about which state had the toughest trees to peck. The Mississippi woodpecker said his state had a tree that no woodpecker had ever been able to peck, and challenged the Texas woodpecker to try it. To the amazement of the Mississippi woodpecker, the Texas woodpecker pecked a hole in the tree with no problem.

Now it was the Texas woodpecker's turn to try and prove that his state had the most impenetrable trees. He told the Mississippi woodpecker that in Texas there was a tree with a bark so hard that no bird had managed to get his beak into it. The Mississippi woodpecker took up the challenge of driving his beak into the tree and, to the dismay of the Texas woodpecker, succeeded easily.

Both woodpeckers were puzzled as to why they were more successful with trees in states other than their own. In the end they concluded that your pecker is always harder when you're away from home.

A male and a female duck were feeling randy on the pond. But when he told her he wanted to mate, she became shy and said there was no way she was doing it in public. Instead, she wanted to be treated like a lady and taken to a hotel.

So he booked them both into a smart hotel for the day. She liked the room, but just as he was preening his feathers ready for action, she announced that there would be no sex unless he wore a condom.

"Where am I going to get a condom?" he demanded.

"Have you no class?" she said. "Ring down for room service. And while you're at it, you can order a round of smoked salmon sandwiches and a pot of Earl Grey."

So the male duck phoned room service. Fifteen minutes later, there was a knock on the door. The male duck answered it to find the room service waiter standing there with a tray of orders.

"Here are your sandwiches, sir," he said, "and your tea, oh, and your condom. Shall I put it on your bill?"

"Certainly not," said the duck. "What do you think I am, a pervert?"

The chicken and the egg were lying in bed after having sex. The chicken sighed happily, fluffed the pillows, and lit up a cigarette. The egg frowned, then rolled out of bed. "Well I guess that answers *that* question!" he muttered.

A female reporter was interviewing a farmer about Mad Cow Disease. "Mr. Brown," she began. "Do you know the causes of this terrible disease?"

"Sure," said the farmer. "Do you know that the bulls only screw the cows once a year . . . ?"

"That's interesting, but what has this got to do with the origins of Mad Cow Disease?"

" . . . And do you know we milk the cows twice a day?"

"Mr. Brown, what exactly is your point?"

"Lady, if I played with your tits twice a day but only screwed you once a year, wouldn't *you* go mad?"

A ventriloquist was driving in the country when he was attracted to a large farm. He asked for and was given a tour.

As he was shown through the barn, the ventriloquist thought he'd have some fun. He proceeded to make one of the horses talk.

The hired hand, wide-eyed with fear, rushed from the barn to find the farmer. "Sam," he shouted, "those animals are talking! If that little sheep says anything about me, it's a damned lie!"

A farmer asked his vet how he could tell whether his pigs were pregnant.

"It's simple," said the vet. "If the pigs are standing up in the morning, they're not pregnant; but if they're rolling in the mud, they are pregnant."

The following morning he looked out of the window to see all of his pigs standing up. So he loaded the pigs into the back of his pickup truck, drove them to the woods, and fucked them all once. He then brought them back to their pen before retiring to bed, tired from the effort.

The next morning he looked out again. The pigs were standing up, so he loaded them into the truck, drove them to the woods, and fucked every pig twice. He then brought them back to the farm before flopping into bed, very tired.

When he woke up the next morning, the first thing he did was look out the window. To his dismay, the pigs were all standing. So he loaded them into the truck, drove them to the woods and fucked them all three times. He then drove them back to the farm and crashed into bed, absolutely exhausted.

The following morning he was too tired to get out of bed, so he asked his wife whether the pigs were standing up or rolling around in the mud.

"Neither," she said. "They're all in the back of the truck, and one's leaning on the horn."

A guy went to the zoo one day, but while he was standing in front of the gorilla enclosure, the wind gusted and got some grit in his eye. As he pulled down his eyelid to dislodge the particle, the gorilla went crazy, bent open the bars, and beat the guy senseless.

When the guy recovered consciousness, the worried zookeeper explained what had happened, revealing that in gorilla language, pulling down your eyelid means, "Fuck you." However, the explanation failed to appease the guy and he vowed revenge.

The next day he purchased two large knives, two party hats, two party horns, and a large sausage. Putting the sausage in his trousers, he hurried to the zoo and went over to the gorilla's cage. He then tossed a knife, a party hat, and a party horn into the gorilla enclosure. Knowing that the great apes are natural mimics, the guy put on the party hat. The gorilla looked at him, looked at the hat lying on the ground, and put it on. Next, the guy picked up the horn and blew on it. The gorilla picked up his horn and did the same. Then the man picked up his knife, whipped the sausage out of his pants, and sliced it neatly in two.

The gorilla looked at the knife in his cage, looked at his own crotch, and pulled down his eyelid.

Q: How do you know if you're really ugly?

A: Dogs hump your leg with their eyes closed.

RIDDLES

Q: If the dove is the bird of peace,
   what is the bird of true love?

A: The swallow.

Q: What's the difference between a
   dog and a fox?

A: About eight beers.

Q: Why is Santa's sack so big?

A: Because he comes only once a year.

Q: What did the cock say to the
   condom?

A: Cover me, I'm going in.

Q: Have you heard about the new super-sensitive condoms?

A: They hang around after the man leaves and talk to the woman.

Q: What do peanut butter and hookers have in common?

A: Both spread for bread.

Q: What do you call a man who cries while he masturbates?

A: A tearjerker.

Q: Why is being in the military like a blow job?

A: The closer you get to discharge, the better you feel.

Q: Why did the army private tattoo sergeant's stripes on his cock?

A: He loved to pull rank.

Q: Did you hear about the army nurse who went to bed eating popcorn?

A: She woke up with a kernel between her legs.

Q: How do you get a sweet little eighty-year-old lady to say "fuck"?

A: Get another sweet little eighty-year-old lady to yell "Bingo."

Q: What did Cinderella do when she got to the ball?

A: Gagged.

Q: How did the Dairy Queen get pregnant?

A: The Burger King didn't cover his whopper.

Q: Have you heard about the new line of tampons with bells and tinsel?

A: It's for the Christmas period.

Q: What two things in the air will get a woman pregnant?

A: Her legs.

Q: Define "Egghead"

A: What Mrs. Dumpty gives to Humpty.

Q: What is 6.9?

A: 69 ruined by a period.

■

Q: Why does it take one million sperm to fertilize one egg?

A: Because they won't stop to ask for directions.

■

Q: Did you hear about the new Viagra eye drops?

A: They make you look hard.

■

Q: Why is a man like a hurricane?

A: Because you never know how big they're going to be or how long they're going to last.

GOOD MEDICINE

A woman with a baby was waiting in the doctor's examining room. After putting the baby on the scales, the doctor found him to be underweight. "Is the baby breast or bottle fed?" he asked.

"Breast fed," replied the woman.

"Right," said the doctor. "Please strip down to your waist."

The woman took off her top, and the doctor pressed, kneaded, rolled, cupped, and pinched both of her breasts. Finally he said: "No wonder the baby is underweight. You don't have any milk."

"I know," she said. "I'm his grandmother. But I'm really pleased I brought him in!"

A young blonde went to a gynecologist and said that she and her husband were desperate to start a family. "We've been trying for months and I just don't seem able to get pregnant," she said.

"I'm sure we can solve your problem," said the gynecologist. "If you'll just take off your underpants and get up on the examining table."

"Well, all right," said the blonde, blushing, "but I'd rather have my husband's baby."

A woman said to her doctor: "Kiss me, kiss me, you handsome brute!"

The doctor replied: "I can't. It wouldn't be ethical. To be honest, I shouldn't be screwing you at all!"

A gorgeous young woman was lying on a gurney in a hospital corridor prior to being taken down to the operating room. A young man in a white coat came over, lifted up the sheet and looked at the girl's naked body before discussing his findings with two other men in white coats. Then the second man lifted up the sheet to examine her. But when the third man came over and lifted the sheet, the young woman lost her temper.

"Are these examinations absolutely necessary?" she demanded.

"I've no idea," said the man. "We're here to paint the ceiling."

An elderly man went to see a urologist who shared an office with several other doctors. The waiting room was full. The receptionist was a large, imposing woman, who said to him in a very loud voice:

"You want to see the doctor about impotence, right?"

All of the other patients' heads turned. Hugely embarrassed, the old man recovered his composure to reply in an equally loud voice: "No, I've come to inquire about a sex change operation—and I'd like the same doctor that did yours!"

One day a horny doctor gave way to temptation and had sex with one of his patients. While it relieved his lust, it made him feel terribly guilty. After work, he went to the bar, and ended up telling the bartender what was troubling him.

"What's the big deal?" said the bartender. "I'm sure she gave consent, right?"

"Well, she couldn't really," replied the doctor, "since I'm a veterinarian."

The Queen of England was on a tour of one of Canada's top hospitals when she passed a room where a male patient was masturbating. "Oh, my!" she exclaimed. "That's disgraceful."

"I'm sorry," said the doctor leading the tour, "but this man has a very serious condition where the testicles fill rapidly with semen. If he doesn't do that five times a day, they would explode and he would most likely die instantly."

"I understand," said the Queen sympathetically. On the next floor they passed a room where a young nurse was giving a patient a blow job. "Oh, my!" gasped the Queen. "What's happening in there?"

The doctor replied: "Same problem, better health care plan."

Having been informed that the husband was infertile, a childless couple decided to try artificial insemination. When the woman arrived at the clinic, she was told to undress, climb on the table, and place her feet in the stirrups. She was feeling very uncomfortable about the whole situation and when the doctor started dropping his pants, she freaked.

"Wait a second! What the hell is going on here?" she yelled.

"Don't you want to get pregnant?" demanded the doctor.

"Well, yes, but . . ."

"Then lie back and spread 'em," ordered the doctor. "We're out of the bottled stuff, so you'll have to make do with what's on tap."

A nervous young man was pacing up and down the waiting room at a maternity hospital. Eventually he asked another guy, who seemed more experienced in these matters: "How long after the baby is born can you have sex with the mother?"

The older guy said: "It depends on whether or not she's in a private room."

A man went to a psychiatrist and said: "Doctor, I suffer from premature ejaculation. Can you help me?"

The psychiatrist said: "No, but I can introduce you to a woman with a short attention span."

A mother asked the gynecologist to examine her teenage daughter. "She has been having some strange symptoms," explained the mother, "and I'm a little worried about her."

The gynecologist examined the girl before announcing: "Madam, I believe your daughter is pregnant."

"That's nonsense!" exclaimed the mother. "My little girl has nothing whatsoever to do with boys. Do you, darling?"

"No, Mom," replied the daughter innocently. "You know that I have never so much as kissed a boy!"

The gynecologist looked at them both. Then silently he stood up and walked over to the window, staring out.

He continued staring out the window until the mother felt compelled to ask, "Doctor, is there something out there?"

"No, Madam," he replied. "It's just that the last time anything like this happened, a star appeared in the East, and I was looking to see if another one was going to show up."

A man suffered serious sunburn after falling asleep on a beach. His wife rushed him to a hospital where the doctor rubbed lotion over him and prescribed Viagra.

"Viagra?" exclaimed the wife. "What good is Viagra in his condition?"

The doctor replied, "It will keep the sheet off him."

DIVINE IRREVERENCE

Two Irishmen were sitting in a bar, watching the entrance to the brothel across the street. A Baptist minister went in, and one of the Irishmen said: "Ah, 'tis a shame to see a man of the cloth goin' bad." Then a rabbi went in, and the Irishman shook his head sadly and remarked: 'Tis a shame to see that the Jews are fallin' victim to temptation." A few minutes later, a Catholic priest went in. "Ah, what a terrible shame," said the Irishman. "One of the girls must be very ill indeed."

ALL
DENOMINATIONS
WELCOME

A Catholic couple was becoming increasingly desperate for a baby. Eventually they asked their priest to pray for them.

The priest said: "I'm going to Rome on a long sabbatical and, while I'm there, I'll light a candle for you at the altar of St. Peter."

When the priest returned to his parish ten months later, he discovered that the woman had given birth to sextuplets. "It's a miracle!" exclaimed the priest. "But I understand your husband has left the country?"

"So he has, Father. He's flown to Rome to blow your damn candle out."

An old priest was getting fed up with the number of people in his parish who were confessing to adultery. One Sunday in the pulpit, he announced: "If I hear one more person confess to adultery, I'm quitting!"

Since he was so popular, the parishioners came up with a code word to avoid incurring his wrath: anyone who had committed adultery would say they had "fallen."

The arrangement appeared to satisfy the old priest right up until his death. His young replacement soon settled into parish life and visited the mayor to express his concern about safety in the town. "You have to do something about the sidewalks," the new priest told the mayor. "When people come into the confessional, they keep talking about having fallen."

A missionary was sent to live with a primitive native tribe that lived in the depths of the jungle. He spent several years with the people, during which time he taught them English, and how to read and write. He also taught them the Christian ways of the white man, and one thing that he stressed in particular was the evil of sexual sin, namely no adultery and no fornication.

One day, the wife of one of the tribe's noblemen gave birth to a child. But to everyone's horror, the child was white. Not surprisingly, this caused a veritable stir in the village. The chief sent for the missionary and said: "You have taught us the evils of sexual sin, but here is a black woman who gives birth to a white child. You are the only white man who has been in the village for many years. What is the explanation?"

The missionary said: "No, my good man, you are mistaken. This is a natural occurrence, what we English call an albino. Nature does this on some occasions. For example, look at that flock of sheep. They are all white except among them, look, there is one black sheep."

The chief thought it over for a moment, called the missionary forward, and whispered in his ear: "OK. Tell you what. You don't say anything about the black sheep, and I won't say anything about the white child."

The Mother Superior in the convent school was chatting with her young charges, and asked them what they wanted to be when they grew up.

A twelve-year-old raised her hand and said, "I want to be a prostitute."

The Mother Superior fainted dead away on the spot. When they revived her, she raised her head from the ground and gasped, "What—did—you—say—?"

The young girl shrugged. "I said I want to be a prostitute."

"A prostitute!" the Mother Superior said. "Oh, praise sweet Jesus! And I thought you said you wanted to be a Protestant."

Sister Mary Catherine and Sister Mary Elizabeth were walking through the park when they were jumped by two thugs. Their habits were ripped from them, and the men sexually assaulted them.

Sister Mary Catherine cast her eyes heavenward and cried: "Forgive him, Lord, for he knows not what he is doing!"

Sister Mary Elizabeth turned and said: "Mine does . . ."

Two nuns decided they would sneak out of the convent for a night on the town. They hit all the bars and dance clubs until, at about two o'clock in the morning, they decided it was time to head back to the convent.

To enter the convent grounds undetected, they had to crawl under some barbed wire. As they started crawling on their bellies beneath the barbed wire, the first nun turned to the second and said: "I feel like a marine."

"Me, too," replied the second nun. "But where are we going to find one at this time of night?"

Stranded for the night, a man sought refuge in a convent. Reluctantly, the Mother Superior allowed him to stay over. "But," she pointed out, "we have ten new nuns who may not yet be strong enough to resist temptation, so you must stay in your room and refrain from any contact whatsoever with the sisters."

The man agreed.

The next morning, after the man had gone, the Mother Superior called all the nuns together for a meeting. "Sisters," she said, "we had a man stay here last night . . ."

Nine nuns gasped, one giggled.

". . . In his room," added the Mother Superior, "we found a used condom . . ."

Nine nuns gasped, one giggled.

". . . And in this condom, we found a hole."

Nine nuns giggled, one gasped.

A woman went to her priest and said, "Father, I have a problem. I have two female parrots, but they only know how to say one thing."

"What do they say?" inquired the priest.

"They say, 'Hi, we're hookers! Do you want to have some fun?'"

"That's obscene," snorted the priest. After thinking for a moment, he said: "I may have a solution to your problem. I have two male talking parrots, which I have taught to pray and read the Bible. Bring your parrots over to my house, and we'll put them in the cage with Francis and Peter. My parrots can teach your parrots to pray and worship, and your birds will soon stop saying that awful phrase."

"Thank you," said the woman. "That sounds like a splendid idea."

So the next day she brought her female parrots to the priest's house. As he ushered her in, she saw that his two male parrots were inside the cage holding rosary beads and praying. Impressed, she walked over and put her parrots in the cage with them. A few minutes later, the female parrots squawked in unison: "Hi, we're hookers! Do you want to have some fun?"

Shocked, one male parrot looked over at the other male parrot and said, "Put the beads away, Francis! Our prayers have been answered."

A young priest got up one morning and went to breakfast. On his way, he passed two nuns and said cheerily: "Good morning, Sisters."

The nuns replied: "You got out on the wrong side of the bed this morning!"

Taken aback by their reply, he walked on and met a monk. "Good morning, Brother," said the priest.

"You got out on the wrong side of the bed this morning!" replied the monk.

Confused, the priest then bumped into a fellow priest. "Good morning, Father," he said.

The other priest said, "You got out on the wrong side of the bed this morning!"

By now the young priest was furious. He continued his walk to the dining hall without greeting anyone. But then the bishop saw him and said: "Father . . ."

The priest glared at the bishop and snapped: "No, I did not get out on the wrong side of the bed this morning!"

The bishop was puzzled. "I don't know what you mean."

The priest realized his mistake. "I am sorry, your holiness. What is it you want?"

The bishop looked at him and said: "All I was going to ask was why you were wearing Sister Mary's shoes."

A doctor was doing the rounds of a maternity ward. "And when is Mrs. Black's baby due?" he asked.

"March 12," replied the nurse.

"Right," said the doctor. "And how about Mrs. White? When is her baby due?"

"She's due on March 12, too," said the nurse.

"Oh, and Mrs. Brown?" asked the doctor.

"She's also due on March 12," said the nurse.

"And Mrs. Green?" said the doctor, raising his eyebrows. "Don't tell me she's due on March 12 as well?"

"I don't think so," said the nurse. "She didn't go on the church picnic."

The pastor entered his donkey in a race and it won. The pastor was so pleased with the donkey that he entered it in another race, and it won again. The local paper read: PASTOR'S ASS OUT FRONT.

The bishop was so upset with this kind of publicity that he ordered the pastor not to enter the donkey in another race. The next day, the local paper headline read: BISHOP SCRATCHES PASTOR'S ASS.

This was too much for the bishop, so he ordered the pastor to get rid of the donkey. The pastor decided to give it to a nun in a nearby convent. The local paper, hearing of the news, posted the following headline the next day: NUN HAS BEST ASS IN TOWN.

The bishop fainted. He informed the nun that she would have to get rid of the donkey, so she sold it to a farmer for $10. The next day the paper read: NUN SELLS ASS FOR $10.

Frustrated, the bishop ordered the nun to buy back the donkey and lead it to the plains where it could run wild. The next day the headlines read: NUN ANNOUNCES HER ASS IS WILD AND FREE.

EMPLOYEE RELATIONS

The secretary walked into her boss's office and announced: "I'm afraid I have some bad news for you."

"Kelly," said the boss, "why do you always bring me bad news? Try to be more positive."

"OK," she said. "The good news is you're not sterile."

■

After telling his wife he was working late at the office, a man took his secretary to a hotel and had wild sex with her. But on his way home, he noticed a huge love bite on his neck and began to panic. What would he tell his wife?

Walking in the door, he was greeted by his excited dog. In a moment of inspiration, he dropped to the floor and pretended to fight off the affectionate dog. Holding his neck with one hand, he went into the living room and exclaimed, "Honey, look what the dog did to my neck!"

His wife jumped up, ripped open her blouse and said: "That's nothing. Look what he did to my tits!"

■

During a staff meeting in Heaven, God, Moses and St. Peter concluded that the behavior of former President Clinton had necessitated the creation of an eleventh commandment. The three worked long and hard in a brainstorming session to try to settle on the wording of the new commandment because they were aware that it should have the same majesty and dignity as the other ten. After many revisions, they finally agreed that the eleventh commandment should be: "Thou shalt not comfort thy rod with thy staff."

Johnny wanted to screw a girl in his office, but she had a boyfriend.

One day Johnny got so frustrated that he went up to her and said, "I'll give you $1,000 if you let me screw you." But the girl said, "NO WAY!" Johnny said, "I'll be fast. I'll throw the money on the floor, you bend down, and I'll be finished by the time you pick it up." She thought for a moment and said that she would have to consult her boyfriend. So she called her boyfriend and told him the story.

Her boyfriend says, "Ask him for $2,000 and pick up the money very fast; he won't even be able to get his pants down!" So she agrees and accepts the proposal.

Half an hour goes by and the boyfriend is waiting for his girlfriend to call. Finally after 45 minutes the boyfriend calls and asks, "What happened?"

She said, "The bastard used coins!"

GROSS ANATOMY

A teenage girl came downstairs for her date wearing a see-through blouse and no bra. Her grandmother went mad.

"Loosen up," said the teenager. "These are modern times. You gotta let your rosebuds show!"

And with that, she left for her date.

The next day the teenager came downstairs to find her granny sitting there with no top on. The sight of granny's wrinkled breasts made the girl want to die, particularly as she was expecting friends to call on her any minute.

"Loosen up," said granny. "If you can show off your rosebuds, then I can display my hanging baskets!"

A flat-chested woman went shopping for a new bra. She tried six shops in search of a size 28A bra, but couldn't find one anywhere. She was just about to give up when she stumbled across a small lingerie shop that was run by an elderly deaf lady.

"Have you got any bras in size 28A?" asked the woman.

"What did you say?" said the old lady.

"Have you got anything in size 28A?" repeated the woman, louder.

"Sorry, I didn't catch that, dear. What is it you want?"

In despair, the woman lifted up her T-shirt to reveal her breasts. "Have you got anything for these?" she asked.

The old lady looked at the woman's breasts and said: "Have you tried Clearasil?"

With a strong wind gusting down the street, a police officer noticed an old woman standing on a corner holding on tightly to her hat while her skirt blew up to her waist.

The cop said: "Hey, lady, while you're holding on to your precious hat, everybody's getting a good look at everything you have."

"Listen, sonny," replied the old woman, "what they're looking at is eighty-five years old. But this hat is brand-new!"

■

Q: What did one saggy boob say to the other saggy boob?

A: If we don't get some support soon, people are going to think we're nuts.

A man phoned the doctor and said in a panic: "A mouse ran up my wife's honeypot."

"Right," said the doctor, "I'll be over in ten minutes. In the meantime, try waving a piece of cheese between her legs to lure it out."

When the doctor arrived, the husband was waving an open can of tuna over the wife's opening.

"What are you doing?" exclaimed the doctor. "I said to use cheese!"

"I know," said the husband. "But I've got to get the cat out first!"

Emma was a new recruit to the red light district. After performing her first trick, she described the experience to the other girls.

"He was a big, muscular marine," she said.

"What did he want to do?" asked the others.

"I told him a straight shag was $100, but he said he didn't have that much. So I told him a blow job would be $75, but he didn't have that much either. He said he only had $25, so I told him that all he could have for $25 was a hand job. He agreed, so I pulled it out. I put one hand on it. Then I put the other hand above that one." Raising her eyebrows and smiling, she continued, "Then I put the first hand above the second hand . . ."

"My God!" exclaimed the others. "It must have been huge! Then what did you do?"

"I loaned him $75!"

A hospital patient recovering from minor surgery was being given an alcohol rub by two of the hospital's more attractive nurses. While manipulating the man's body they noted that the word *tiny* was tattooed on the head of his penis.

Some months after the man's discharge, Mary, one of the nurses, told Joan, the other, that she had dated their former patient.

"How could you go out with a man who had 'tiny' tattooed on his love stick?" exclaimed Joan.

"How could I indeed!" said Mary. "It said 'tiny' when it was quiet, but when I aroused it, it spelled out 'Tiny's Delicatessen and Catering Service. We deliver at all times, twenty-four hours a day!'"

Reviewing his regiment, the colonel could not help noticing that one of the soldiers had a huge erection. "Give this man thirty days' leave to go home to his wife," he told the sergeant major.

A few months later, the same man was again sporting a huge erection on the parade ground. "Sergeant major!" said the colonel. "Give this man another thirty days' leave."

Two months later, exactly the same thing happened. This time the colonel was angry. "Sergeant major, haven't we given this man two periods of leave?"

"Yes, sir," replied the sergeant major.

"Then what's the problem?" demanded the colonel. "Why has he got that huge erection again?"

The sergeant major whispered: "I think it's you he's fond of, sir."

A virgin wanted to marry a farmer boy. One day she went to his parents' house for dinner and afterward they were walking through the fields when she saw two horses mating.

"What are they doing?" she asked.

"They're making love," said the boy.

"What's that long thing he's sticking in there?"

"Oh, uh, that's his rope."

"Well, what are those two round things on the other end?"

"Er, those are his knots."

"OK, OK," said the girl, happy with the explanation. "I get it."

As they continued to stroll, they came to a barn and went in. The girl announced: "I want you to make love to me the way those animals were."

Excited and surprised, he readily agreed, but suddenly she grabbed his balls and squeezed them hard.

"Whoa! What are you doing?" he shrieked in pain.

"I'm untying the knots so I'll get more rope."

A man is in a hotel lobby. As he turns to go to the front desk, he accidentally bumps into a woman beside him and as he does, his elbow goes into her breast.

They are both quite startled. The man turns to her and says, "Ma'am, if your heart is as soft as your breast, I know you'll forgive me."

She replies, "If your penis is as hard as your elbow, I'm in room 436."

A guy was nervous about making a move on his new girlfriend because he thought his penis was rather on the small side. So he asked his friend for advice. The friend said: "Don't worry. Just get her in the mood and everything will be fine. I'm sure she won't think your dick is small."

So on their next date the guy drove his girl-friend to a secluded spot. After kissing her tenderly, he plucked up the courage to open the zipper on his jeans and guide her hand down onto his organ.

"No thanks," said the girl. "I don't smoke."

A man was sitting on a train opposite a girl in a short skirt. Although he tried not to stare, he couldn't take his eyes off her, particularly when it became obvious that she wasn't wearing any underpants. Realizing what was going on, she asked him: "Are you looking at my pussy?"

"Er, yes. I'm sorry."

"It's OK," said the girl. "My pussy's very talented. Watch this. I'll make it blow a kiss to you."

Sure enough, it blew a kiss at him.

"That's not all," she boasted. "I can also make it wink."

Sure enough, she made it wink at him.

"Come and sit next to me," she said, patting the seat. "Would you like to stick a couple of fingers in?"

"My God!" said the man. "Can it whistle, too?"

A man walked into the doctor's office and said: "Doctor, I have five penises."

"I see," said the doctor. "How do your trousers fit?"

"Like a glove."

One Monday morning a mailman was walking the neighborhood on his usual route. As he approached one of the homes he noticed that both cars were in the driveway. His wonder was cut short by Bob, the homeowner, coming out with a load of empty beer and liquor bottles.

"Wow Bob, it looks like you guys had one hell of a party last night," the mailman commented.

Bob, in obvious pain, replied, "Actually we had it Saturday night. This is the first I have felt like moving since 4:00 o'clock Sunday morning. We had about fifteen couples from around the neighborhood over for some weekend fun and it got a bit wild. Hell, we got so drunk around midnight that we started playing WHO AM I?"

The mailman thought a moment and asked, "How do you play that?"

"Well, all the guys go in the bedroom and we come out one at a time with a sheet covering us and only our 'privates' showing through a hole in the sheet. Then the women try to guess who it is."

The mailman laughed and said, "Damn, I'm sorry I missed that."

"Probably a good thing you did," Bob responded. "Your name came up seven times...."

A guy picked up a girl and took her back to his hotel room. She turned out to be a raving nymphomaniac and, after six times, she was still screaming for more. Eventually, after the eighth time, he said he needed to go out and buy some cigarettes.

On his way, he stopped at the men's room. Standing in front of the urinal, he unzipped, but couldn't find his dick. After fishing around for it for a minute, he said: "Look, it's OK. She's not here!"

The newly born sperm was receiving instructions in conception. The instructor said: "As soon as you hear the siren, run for the tunnel and swim in a straight line until you reach the entrance of a damp cavern. At the end of the cavern you will find a red, sticky ball, which is the egg. Address it and say, "I'm a sperm." She will answer, "I'm the egg." From that moment on, you will work together to create the embryo. Do you understand?"

The sperm nodded in the affirmative, and the instructor said: "Then good luck, chaps!"

Three days later, the sperm was taking a nap when he heard the siren. He woke up immediately and ran to the tunnel. A multitude of sperm swam behind him. He knew he had to arrive first. When he was near the entrance to the cavern, he looked back and saw that he was way ahead. Then he was able to swim at a slower pace until he reached the red, sticky ball. When, at last, he got to the red, sticky ball, he brightened up, smiled, and said: "Hi, I'm a sperm."

The red, sticky ball smiled and said: "Hi, I'm a tonsil."

POLITICALLY INCORRECT

After an evening of drinking, a guy and his Chinese girlfriend ended up in his bedroom.

"What do you want to do?" she asked. "I'm up for anything."

"Well, in that case," he whispered, "what I'd really like is a 69."

"Forget it," she said. "There's no way I'm cooking chicken chow mein at this time of night."

When her husband had to cancel his vacation to the Caribbean because of business commitments, a wife decided to go alone. Making the most of her freedom, she allowed herself to be seduced by a black man. After a passionate night of sex, she asked him his name.

"I'm not going to tell you," he said, "because you'll laugh."

"No, I won't," she said.

"You will."

"I won't—I promise."

"OK, my first name is Snow."

The woman immediately started laughing.

"I knew you'd make fun of it!" he said.

"No, it's just that my husband won't believe me when I tell him that I had ten inches of Snow every day in the Caribbean!"

A beautiful assistant to a leading New York banker was given the task of entertaining an important Chinese client on his visit to the Big Apple. The evening went so well that at the end of it, much to her surprise, the client asked her to marry him.

Remembering what her boss had told her about not hurting the client's feelings at any cost, she decided not to reject him outright. So she tried to think of a way of dissuading the little man from wanting to marry her. After a few moments' thought, she announced: "I will only agree to marry you on three conditions. First, I want my engagement ring to have a huge diamond with a matching diamond tiara."

The Chinese man nodded his head enthusiastically. "No problem. I buy, I buy."

Realizing that her first condition was too easy, she then said: "Second, I want a chateau built in the middle of champagne country in France."

The Chinese man paused to think for a while. Then he whipped out his mobile phone, called brokers in New York and France before nodding to the woman. "OK, I build, I build."

Aware that she had just one condition left, the assistant knew she had better make it a really tough one. So she said: "Since I simply adore to have sex, I want the man I marry to have a twelve-inch penis."

The little Chinese man looked distraught, and sank to his knees, all the while muttering to himself in his native tongue. Finally, shaking his head in despair, he said to the woman, "All right. I cut, I cut."

Two Italian virgins were on the first night of their honeymoon. They had no idea what they were supposed to do, so he called his mother for help.

"Just cuddle up to each other," advised Mama, "and let nature take its course."

They cuddled up on the bed, but nothing happened, so a few minutes later he phoned his mother again.

"Get into bed," she suggested. "Kiss each other and see where it leads."

So they got into bed and kissed, but still nothing happened. So he phoned his mother for a third time.

Frustrated, Mama replied: "Listen, just take the biggest thing you have and stick it in the hairiest thing she has."

Ten minutes later her son called her back and said hesitantly, "Right, I have my nose in her armpit. Now what do I do?"

A cowboy was riding through the desert when he came across an Indian who was lying on the ground with his dick hanging out.

"What are you doing?" inquired the cowboy.

"Me tell time," said the Indian. "Penis act as sundial."

The cowboy was intrigued. "So what time do you make it?"

"11:08."

"Me, too. That's amazing."

Impressed with the Indian's ingenuity, the cowboy rode off and a few miles further on he stumbled across another Indian lying on the ground with his dick out.

"I know what you're up to," said the cowboy. "You're telling the time. What time do you make it?"

The Indian studied the shadow from his penis. "11:21."

"That's right," said the cowboy. "Unbelievable!"

The cowboy rode off until a few miles further on he spotted another Indian lying on the ground with his dick out. But this time the Indian was jerking himself off.

"What the heck are you doing?" asked the cowboy.

"Me winding clock."

Maria had just gotten married and, being a traditional Italian, she was still a virgin. On her wedding night, staying at her mother's house, she was very nervous. Her mother reassured her, "Don't worry, Maria, Tony's a good man. Go upstairs and he'll take care of you. Meanwhile, I'll be making pasta."

So, up she went. When she got upstairs, Tony took off his shirt and exposed his hairy chest. Maria ran downstairs to her mother and said, "Mama, Mama, Tony's got a big hairy chest!"

"Don't worry, Maria," said the mother. "All good men have hairy chests. Go upstairs. He'll take good care of you."

So, up she went again. When she got up to the bedroom, Tony took off his pants, exposing his hairy legs. Again, Maria ran downstairs to her mother. "Mama, Mama, Tony took off his pants, and he's got hairy legs!"

"Don't worry! All good men have hairy legs. Tony's a good man. Go upstairs and he'll take good care of you."

So, up she went again. When she got there, Tony took off his socks and on his left foot he was missing three toes. When Maria saw this, she ran downstairs.

"Mama, Mama, Tony's got a foot and a half!"

Her mama said, "Stay here and stir the pasta."

A pilot, a lawyer, three Boy Scouts, and a priest were on a plane that was going down, but there were only three parachutes. "Give them to the Boy Scouts," said the pilot. "They're young and have their whole lives in front of them."

"Fuck the Boy Scouts," said the lawyer.

"Do we have time?" asked the priest.

Three hookers were comparing notes about their customers from the night before.

"I entertained a cowboy last night," said the first.

"How did you know he was a cowboy?" asked the others.

"Well, he wore a cowboy hat, cowboy boots, and kept both the hat and the boots on all the time we were together."

"Sounds like a cowboy, all right," agreed the others.

"I entertained a lawyer," announced the second. "I could tell because he wore a three-piece suit and packed a briefcase. He wore the vest of the suit and hung on to the briefcase all the time."

The others agreed he sounded like a lawyer.

"I had a farmer for a client," said the third.

"How did you know he was a farmer?" asked the others.

"First he complained it was too dry, then he whined that it was too wet, then he asked if he could pay me in the fall."

A rabbi kept a jar full of foreskins on his desk as mementos of the many circumcisions that he had performed over the years. One day he took the foreskins to a leatherworker and asked him what he could do with them. The leatherworker said: "Come back in two days."

The rabbi returned two days later, and the leatherworker presented him with a wallet. "One lousy wallet!" snorted the rabbi. "Was that all you could make out of that entire jar of foreskins?"

"Listen," said the leatherworker. "You rub it a little bit, and it turns into a briefcase."

ORAL AGREEMENTS

"Good afternoon, ladies," said Sherlock Holmes to three women sitting on a London park bench.

"Do you know those women?" asked his faithful companion, Dr. Watson.

"No," said Holmes, as the pair continued walking. "I don't know the spinster, the prostitute, and the new bride."

"Good Heavens, Holmes! If you don't know them, how can you be so sure that they are what you say?"

"Elementary, my dear Watson," explained Holmes, glancing back. "Do you see how they are eating bananas?"

"So?"

"Well, Watson, the spinster holds the banana in her left hand and uses her right hand to break the banana into small pieces which she puts into her mouth."

"I see what you mean, Holmes. That's amazing! What about the prostitute?"

"She holds the banana in both hands and crams it into her mouth."

"Holmes, you've surpassed yourself! But how do you know the other woman is a new bride?"

"Simple," said Holmes. "She holds the banana in her left hand and uses her right hand to push her head toward the banana."

Q: What is the speed limit for sex?

A: 68, because at 69 you have to turn around.

A young couple headed up to the wilds of Canada for a romantic weekend. The guy went off to chop wood but returned after twenty minutes, complaining that his hands were cold.

"That's OK," said his girlfriend. "You can warm them between my thighs."

So he slipped his icy hands between her warm thighs before going back to his wood chopping. A few minutes later he was back again, complaining that his hands were cold. Once more, she let him warm them between her thighs before he resumed his work in the forest. Five minutes later, he returned again.

"My hands are so cold," he said. "Can I warm them between your thighs?"

His girlfriend glared at him. "Don't your ears ever get cold?"

Little Jenny came home from playing at Dean's house and called out: "Hey, mom. Guess what! Dean's got a penis like a peanut!"

Her mother was understandably confused for a second, then queried: "What, you mean— it's shaped like a peanut?"

"No, silly . . . it tastes salty!"

HUSBAND: I fancy kinky sex. How about I come in your ear?

WIFE: No, I might go deaf.

HUSBAND: I've been coming in your mouth for twenty years, and you're still talking!

A horny guy went to a whorehouse but had only five dollars. He was thrown out of the first two places he tried, so he visited a third.

"I need a blow job," he told the Madame. "But I've only got five dollars."

"OK," she said. "That's not much, but for five dollars we can give you a penguin."

"What's a penguin?" he asked.

"You'll see."

So he paid his five dollars, went upstairs and waited for his penguin. A few minutes later a young woman came and gave him a blow job. But just as he was about to come, she suddenly stopped and walked away. Frustrated beyond belief, he waddled after her with his pants around his ankles, screaming: "What's a penguin?"

A man went to a tattoo parlor and had the words "yes" and "no" tattooed on his dick. When he got home, he stripped and showed his wife the aroused organ and its new tattoo.

"What do you think?" he asked.

"What do I think?" she yelled. "You tell me how to cook, you tell me how to dress, you tell me how to wear my hair, you tell me how to clean the house . . . and now you're gonna put words in my mouth!"

A man and a woman were waiting at the hospital donation center.

The man decided to strike up a conversation and asked her: "What are you here for?"

"I'm here to donate some blood," she replied. "They're giving me five dollars for it."

"Right," said the man. I'm actually here to donate sperm. But they pay me $25."

The woman looked thoughtful for a moment and they chatted some more before going their separate ways. A couple of months later, the same man and woman met again at the donation center.

"Hi," he called out. "Here to donate blood again?"

The woman shook her head with her mouth closed: "Unh, unh."

A guy entered a clock and watch shop and saw the most gorgeous female clerk behind the counter. He calmly walked up to her, unzipped his pants, and flopped his dick out onto the counter.

"What are you doing, sir?" she asked. "This is a clock shop!"

"I know," he said, "and I'd like two hands and a face put on this!"

"Why on earth do you want a tattoo of a $100 bill on your penis?" asked the artist.

The man explained: "First, I like to play with money. Second, I like to watch the money grow. And third, and most importantly, the next time my wife wants to blow $100, she can stay home to do it."

UNDERAGED

A little girl came running into the house in tears.

"Mommy, I need a glass of cider. Quick!"

"Why?" asked her mother.

"Because I cut my hand on a thorn and I want the pain to go away."

The mother reached for the bottle, but was still puzzled by the request. "What makes you think this will work?" she said.

"Because I overheard my big sister saying that whenever she gets a prick in her hand, she can't wait to get it in cider."

Jack and Jenny were twins who couldn't find dates to the prom. So Jenny asked Jack to go with her, but Jack wasn't too keen on the idea.

"No, you're my sister," he said. "That's gross." But, as the day of the prom drew nearer and he still hadn't found another date, he reluctantly agreed to take Jenny to the dance.

As they stood by the punch bowl at the prom, Jenny asked Jack to dance with her. "No," said Jack. "You're my sister. That's gross." But Jenny persuaded him and they had fun.

After the dance, Jenny asked Jack to drive her to Makeout Hill. "No," he said. "You're my sister. It would be gross."

Jenny promised that they would just talk, so Jack relented. They were at Makeout Hill talking when Jenny moved to the back seat and said, "Come on, Jack, take me."

This time, Jack didn't argue. When he moved on top of Jenny, she murmured, "You're a lot lighter than Dad."

Jack said, "I know. Mom told me last night."

▩

Two poor kids went to a birthday party at a rich kid's house. The birthday boy was so rich that he had his own swimming pool and all the kids went in. As they were changing afterward, one of the poor kids said to the other one: "Did you notice how small the rich kid's penis was?"

"Yeah," said his friend. "It's probably because he's got toys to play with."

A little boy went up to his dad and asked: "Dad, what's the difference between potentially and realistically?"

His father replied: "Well, son, go ask your mother if she would sleep with Robert Redford for a million dollars. Then ask your sister if she would sleep with Brad Pitt for a million dollars. Finally, ask your brother if he would sleep with Tom Cruise for a million dollars."

So the boy went up to his mom and asked her if she would sleep with Robert Redford for a million dollars. "My God, of course I would," she said. "He's good looking."

Then the boy asked his sister if she would sleep with Brad Pitt for a million dollars. "Are you kidding?" she said. "Of course I would. He's so gorgeous."

Finally the boy asked his brother if he would sleep with Tom Cruise for a million dollars.

"I sure would," replied the brother. "Who wouldn't for a million bucks?"

So the boy went back to his dad and said: "I think I learned the difference between potentially and realistically."

"So what's the difference?" asked the father.

"Well, potentially we're sitting on three million dollars; realistically we're living with two sluts and a fag!"

It was the first day of a new school year. Three boys arrived late for class, and the teacher asked the first boy: "Why are you late?"

The boy replied: "I've been on Honeysuckle Hill."

"Take your seat," said the teacher.

Then she asked the second boy why he was late.

"I've also been on Honeysuckle Hill."

And when the teacher asked the third boy why he was late, he gave the same answer. As the boys were sitting down, a girl walked in to class.

"Let me guess," said the teacher. "You too were on Honeysuckle Hill?"

"No," the girl replied. "I *am* Honeysuckle Hill."

OVER THE HILL

An old couple was on their honeymoon. While she slipped into bed in her skimpiest nightdress, he went into the bathroom. After he had been in there for fifteen minutes, she thought she had better see what he was doing. She found him struggling to put on a condom.

"Why are you putting on a condom?" she asked. "I'm eighty-two. I can't get pregnant!"

"Yes," he said, "but you know how dampness affects my arthritis."

A family is sitting around the dinner table. The son asks his father, "Dad, how many kinds of breasts are there?"

The father, surprised, answers, "Well, son, there are three kinds of breasts. In her twenties, a woman's breasts are like melons: round and firm. In her thirties to forties, they are like pears: still nice but hanging a bit. After fifty, they are like onions."

"Onions?"

"Yes, you see them and they make you cry."

The daughter glares at her father, then asks, "Mom, how many kinds of penises are there?"

The mother, surprised, smiles and replies, "Well dear, a man goes through three phases. In a man's twenties, his penis is like an oak tree, mighty and hard. In his thirties and forties it's like a birch, flexible but reliable. After his fifties, it is like a Christmas tree."

"A Christmas tree?" asks the girl.

"Yes," says the mother. "Dead from the root up and the balls are for decoration only."

An elderly man complained to the doctor of feeling tired. The doctor asked him if he had done anything unusual lately.

The old man said: "Wednesday night, I picked up a twenty-year-old secretary and nailed her three times. Thursday, I hit on a nineteen-year-old waitress; Friday, I made out with an eighteen-year-old friend of my granddaughter; and Saturday, I was lured to a motel by seventeen-year-old twins."

The doctor said: "I hope you took precautions."

"Sure," replied the old man. "I gave 'em all phony names."

A couple that had been married for thirty-five years had just celebrated their sixtieth birthdays. To mark the occasion, a fairy appeared and granted them a wish.

The wife said: "I'd like to spend six months in a hot country."

And POOF! She was given two tickets to Australia.

Then it was the husband's turn. Somewhat hesitantly, he said: "I'd like to have a woman thirty years younger than me."

And POOF! He was ninety.

An eighty-five-year-old man married a twenty-five-year-old woman and, because of his age, she decided that on their wedding night they should have separate suites in case he overdid things.

Nevertheless she expected some form of sexual activity and, sure enough, after a few minutes there was a knock on her door. Her new husband came in, they had sex, and then he said good-night and retired to his suite across the corridor.

Ten minutes later, he was back again. She was surprised, but happily consented to more sex, after which he bade her good-night and returned to his suite.

Fifteen minutes later, just as she was settling down for the night, there was another knock on her door. Once again, it was her husband, wanting yet more sex. Stunned by his voracious appetite, she gladly gave in, and afterward told him: "I'm really impressed that a guy your age has enough juice to go for it three times."

The old man looked puzzled and asked, "Was I here before?"

A couple of ninety-somethings had a one-night stand. Afterward the man thought to himself, "Geez, if I knew she was a virgin I would've been more gentle."

And the woman thought, "Gosh, if I knew he could actually get it up. I would have taken off my panty hose."

PORNUCOPIA

Delivering a crusading speech against porn videos, a mayoral candidate stormed: "I rented one of these cassettes and was shocked to find five acts of oral sex, three of sodomy, a transsexual making love to a dog, and a woman accommodating five men at once. If elected, I will ban such filth. Any questions?"

Half a dozen people shouted, "Where did you rent the tape?"

As the waitress approached the table of foreign businessmen, she noticed them with their hands under the table, frantically jerking off. "Excuse me," she said, "but could you tell me what you're doing with your hands in your pants?"

One of the businessmen zipped up and replied, "Menu says, first come, first served."

On vacation in Morocco, a couple was accosted by a street trader selling footwear. When the husband began admiring a pair of sandals, the trader unleashed his full sales pitch, telling the man that he would become a sex god if he wore them.

Naturally, the man was skeptical. "How can wearing a pair of sandals possibly turn me into a sex god?" he challenged.

"Try them on, try them on," insisted the trader.

"Well, it wouldn't do any harm," smiled the customer's wife.

So the man put on the sandals, and was immediately overcome with intense feelings of sexual desire. But instead of lusting after women, he suddenly fancied the Moroccan and rushed at the startled trader.

The Moroccan screamed: "You've got them on the wrong feet!"

A classical guitarist was hired to play two solos in a movie. After the sessions he was paid handsomely and promised by the director that he would be notified when the movie was released. Three months later he was told that the movie would be making its debut at a porno house in Times Square. Although the venue was not exactly what he had been hoping for, he was determined to attend but decided to wear a raincoat and dark glasses just in case anyone recognized him. Unaccustomed as he was to porno theaters, he sat in the back row next to an elderly couple.

The movie was grossly explicit. There were scenes of oral intercourse, anal intercourse, golden showers, sado-masochism, and near the end a dog had intercourse with the film's leading lady. The guitarist, who was hugely embarrassed by the whole thing, turned to the elderly couple and explained: "I wrote the score and I just came to hear the music."

To which the elderly woman whispered in reply: "We just came to see our dog."

Little Red Riding Hood was on her way to see her grandmother in the forest. Her mother warned her, "Don't walk through the forest. Take the path, or else the Big Bad Wolf will catch you and suck your tits dry!"

Little Red Riding Hood started toward her grandmother's house, but decided to take the shortcut through the forest anyway. A turtle stopped Little Red Riding Hood and warned her, "Turn back and use the path, because if the Big Bad Wolf finds you, he'll suck your tits dry!"

Little Red Riding Hood was almost there, so she kept going through the forest. Sure enough, the Big Bad Wolf jumped out of nowhere and growled, "Take off your shirt

Little Red Riding Hood. I'm gonna suck your tits dry!!"

"Oh no, you don't!" yelled Little Red Riding Hood, as she pulled up her skirt. "You're gonna eat me just like the story says!"